Seasons of my Garden

A Two–Year Recordkeeper

Virginia Lopez Begg

Illustrations by Andrea Brooks

FRIEDMAN/FAIRFAX
PUBLISHERS

A FRIEDMAN/FAIRFAX BOOK

Library of Congress Cataloging-in-Publication data available upon request

ISBN 1-56799-692-2

Editor: Susan Lauzau
Art Director: Jeff Batzli
Designer: Andrea Karman
Production Manager: Camille Lee

Color separations by Bright Arts Graphics (S) Pte Ltd
Printed in Hong Kong by Midas Printing Limited

1 3 5 7 9 10 8 6 4 2

For bulk purchases and special sales, please contact:
Friedman/Fairfax Publishers
Attention: Sales Department
15 West 26th Street
New York, New York 10010
212/685-6610   FAX 212/685-1307

Visit our website:
http://www.metrobooks.com

Contents

Introduction

WHY KEEP A GARDEN JOURNAL?

Like a winding path through a lovely garden, a garden journal allows you to look back at the earlier days of your garden, to notice the details of where you are now, and to imagine your garden as you hope it will unfold in the future. As you record notes and sketch ideas, your garden journal will become a vital and intimate part of the creative process.

This book, however, is a special kind of garden journal. It not only invites you to record your garden's plantings and design, but, like a trusted friend, it also offers helpful guidance on how to make your garden the special place you want it to be. Here you will find many useful suggestions, born of long experience, that will assist you as you move ever closer toward that garden which each of us holds as a private ideal.

With the beginning of each year's section, you'll find space to make notes on goals for the coming gardening season, or you may wish to include a photograph of your garden in all its glory. A weekly diary allows for three years of garden records, offering ample space to make plans for your garden and record its progress. Here you can jot reminders of tasks you wish to complete each week, note successes and failures, detail weather conditions, and keep track of what was planted when. The two-year format encourages you to plot your gardening chores and objectives for the coming years. Use the pages like an engagement calendar, writing in dates for setting out seedlings and notes of particular chores for each week. Graph pages allow you to sketch your garden each year, designing for the future even as you record your present landscape.

A special guide, The Garden's Design (pages 116–120), takes you through the design process in simple, easy-to-follow steps. Every garden, grand or intimate, has two major components to its design. Layout is the first of these. How have you structured your garden? What changes would you like to make? The second includes those things that compose the design: its plantings and its man-made elements, such as paths, walls, and garden ornaments. Whether you are gardening on a brand new plot of raw earth or in a centuries-old garden, it will be helpful to consider these factors as you go through the design process. This process will help you better understand how to record the layout, plantings, and other elements of your garden, and to make exciting plans for the future. Both novices and accomplished gardeners will find lots of tips on making the garden a special place, and the instructions for creating a design provide even the most inexperienced gardeners with a manageable way to begin planning their outdoor spaces.

Practical garden checklists, arranged according to the four seasons, follow the introduction. Here you will find reminders of essential tasks, as well as fresh ideas for improving your garden. Pages for recording plantings (pages 121–125) let you make useful notes on what plants perform well and allow you to keep track of important details like bloom time, when the plants were last divided, and so on.

This journal is designed to be flexible, so that each gardener can adapt it to his or her own specific needs. Be sure to notice the garden suggestions located throughout the recordkeeper section for tips on container gardening, tools you should own, and much more. A map of plant hardiness zones concludes the book; with this handy map you can easily determine the zone in which you live, allowing you to choose plants appropriate for your climate.

Enjoy your garden journal. It is certain to become a pleasurable and invaluable aid as you make real your unique garden vision.

A Year in the Garden

Season-by-Season Checklists

Each year we attend to many of the same tasks in the garden, while we also develop special projects slated for various years. The following lists will remind you of essential chores, as well as provide ideas you may not have considered. Make sure to record your ideas and note important tasks in the weekly diary pages.

WINTER

Winter, that season in which most of our gardens seem quietly at rest, is when the gardener's year really begins. Use the following checklist to help organize your winter gardening chores.

_____ Photograph your garden in winter. It is then that the bones of the garden show best, and both assets and drawbacks reveal themselves. Ask yourself if your garden has enough winter interest in plantings and design.

_____ Notice attractive plants in other gardens and public spaces in your community. List in your garden journal those you might like to add to your garden.

_____ Record in a few words the sum of each winter's weather. This will guide you in future planting and design decisions.

_____ Sketch or list changes to your garden plan that you hope to make in the coming year. These can be as major as a new perennial border or as minor as finials on fence posts.

_____ Collect garden catalogs of every sort, those that feature ornaments and utilitarian items as well as those that offer plants. Make your lists, order early to avoid disappointment, and record your purchases in your garden journal.

_____ Sharpen and clean garden tools, and purchase new tools. Winter is also a good time for painting and repairing garden ornaments that have been brought inside.

_____ If storms occur, pick up debris and prune jagged branches. This will help to keep the winter garden healthy and attractive.

_____ Winter reveals the architecture of trees. Make note of necessary pruning, and do the work now. If you do not do your own pruning, certified arborists often have more time in the dormant season.

_____ Press frost-heaved plants firmly into the ground. Add protective mulch if this continues to be a problem.

_____ Start seeds indoors. See Growing Plants from Seed on pages 30–31.

SPRING

For the gardener, spring is the busiest and most exciting season of the year. Your garden journal will be invaluable as you dig and plant, and make real the garden you have thought about all winter. Following is a checklist to help you keep track of spring tasks.

_____ Remove protective mulch after the danger of a hard freeze has passed. Level frost-heaved garden ornaments such as sundials. Create your own to-do list in your journal as a helpful guide for your spring energy.

_____ Record the spring weather. A few brief words in your journal each season will build a picture of your property's microclimate.

_____ Photograph your garden at its spring peak. This will help to remind you of changes you may like to make in plantings or design.

_____ Fertilize perennial gardens early. Gently cultivate a light scattering of 5-10-10 fertilizer into the top few inches of the soil. Add organic material such as compost or well-rotted manure. Most annuals, vegetables, and other herbaceous plants will benefit from similar feeding.

_____ Divide perennials early and water well after the operation. See Transplanting and Dividing on pages 78–79.

_____ Fertilize trees and shrubs for peak performance, especially those that flower or have been recently planted.

_____ Fertilize the lawn and plant new grass seed in bare patches if necessary. Record your lawn's size and requirements in your garden journal.

_____ Add organic material, fertilizer, and other amendments to soil (soil can be worked in spring when it crumbles easily after being made into a ball). Note in your journal how much material you use so you do not have to guess next year. You can also jot down the dates of these tasks for future planning.

_____ For each plant you add, record the following in your journal: botanical name; common name; cost and where it was purchased; how many you planted; where you planted it (note this on the plan or in words); when it flowered; color of flowers or foliage; any special requirements.

_____ Record good color combinations and comments such as "emerges late in spring." Reminders about the quality of a plant's flowers and foliage can affect later design decisions as well.

_____ Continue to record design changes as you make them, as well as those you would like to make in the future.

_____ Paint arbors, fences, and other architectural features.

_____ Scrub the birdbath and keep it filled with clean water to attract birds.

_____ Edge all planting areas that adjoin lawn. Tidy edges are the secret to a serene landscape.

SUMMER

Summer is the season in which it is pleasant to slow down a bit and enjoy the beauty you have created. If you like, you can certainly continue to plan and plant, but the key ingredient of a beautiful garden in summer is maintenance. Use the following checklist to guide you in your summer chores.

_____ Photograph your garden frequently, both long views and vignettes. Photos will help you remember what is worth repeating and what needs replacement.

_____ Record the general weather conditions. Weather explains much of our garden success, or, occasionally, distress. Learn to garden with your climate, rather than in a constant battle against it.

_____ Water regularly, as permitted in your area, and plant according to available water resources. If you live in an arid climate, become acquainted with the riches of your native flora and of other dry climates.

_____ Mulch to maintain soil moisture and an even soil temperature, as well as to keep down weeds. Roughly ground garden waste, such as last year's leaves, makes good mulch that will add much to the quality of your soil. Otherwise, choose the least expensive locally available material that most resembles the soil itself. Lay the mulch two inches (5cm) thick on flower beds, and about four inches (10cm) thick around shrubs and trees. Keep mulch away from direct contact with bark.

_____ Deadhead flowers as blooms fade. This practice will help to keep your garden fresh and attractive, and will also prevent seed formation that drains energy from the plant. Try to deadhead flowering shrubs as well for better performance next year.

_____ Fertilize annuals and containers once a week with liquid fertilizer. Perennials grown in good soil with compost and a spring addition of 5-10-10 fertilizer should not need further feeding.

_____ Weed! The best way to handle this irksome task is to mentally divide your garden into manageable sections and to weed one section in each gardening session.

_____ Edge all flower and shrub beds at regular intervals. Tidy edges create a feeling of order, serenity, and calm.

_____ Don't forget to mow the lawn. Even if your lawn is far less than perfect, evenly sheared grass enhances all your other plantings. If lawn maintenance takes too much of your time, consider replacing grass with low-growing, evergreen groundcovers and shrubs.

AUTUMN

Autumn glories in its own unique beauty, both in your garden and in the surrounding landscape. The following checklist will assist you in enhancing your garden's late-season appeal, as well as in preparing for winter.

_____ Photograph your garden at the height of the autumn show.

_____ Record the weather for the season. Be especially aware of an overly dry season, and continue watering if necessary.

_____ If desired, plant perennials (peonies, especially, should be planted in autumn) and shrubs; be sure to water well until the ground freezes and mulch after the freeze.

_____ Plant bulbs. See Bulbs on pages 108–109.

_____ Rake leaves from the lawn regularly so they do not smother the grass. Leaves can be left on flower beds and among shrubs as a natural mulch.

_____ Cut off diseased or pest-ridden foliage and put it out with the trash to minimize future problems. All other garden debris should be composted, if at all possible. Just make a pile in a hidden corner, and time will do the rest. Compost is invaluable for good soil and for mulch.

_____ Cut back perennials to a few inches (centimeters) for a tidy look, or leave as they are to form their own protective mulch. If you decide to cut them back, you will have to provide mulch for some, including those that have been recently planted, are shallow-rooted, or are exposed to winter's low afternoon sun. Also provide mulch for semi-evergreen perennials, such as hellebores and big-root geraniums.

_____ Empty flowerpots into the compost pile, soil and all. Gardeners in milder climates may prefer to change the plantings to reflect the seasons.

_____ In freezing climates, store pots, containers, and garden ornaments in a garage or basement to protect them from the weather. This is especially important with terra-cotta, wood, or any other feature that holds water, such as a container or birdbath.

_____ Drain hoses and put them away.

Year

_____

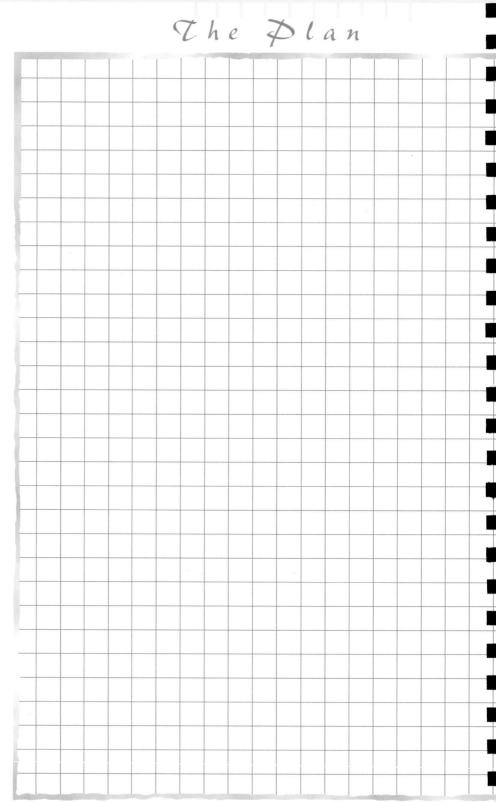

Week One

Week Two

JANUARY

year one

Week Three

Week Four

year
one JANUARY

Week One

Week Two

Week Three

A Garden Tool Basket

Late winter is the perfect time to gather the items you will need to fill a garden tool basket. Good gardening requires good tools, and at this time of year both stores and catalogs are fully supplied. Choose a tool basket of heavy-duty plastic that may be occasionally hosed out and make sure that it is brightly colored, so you can find it easily among your plants. Your basket should also have a sturdy handle for convenient toting. When not in use, store your garden tool basket in an accessible place. You will find yourself doing garden chores much more readily if everything you need is right at hand. Take a moment now to list in your garden journal the items you will want to purchase. Among the items to consider are:

Week Four

❦ A *trowel* and *hand cultivator*. They should fit your hand comfortably and be the best quality you can afford.

❦ *Hand pruners* and *shears*. Quality is critical here as well.

❦ Rust-proof *scissors* are endlessly useful for deadheading and pruning delicate plants and for many other garden chores.

❦ *Twine* and *plastic ties*.

❦ *Plant labels* and an *indelible marking pen*.

❦ Several pairs of inexpensive *garden gloves*, so you can put on a fresh pair when the first get wet and muddy.

❦ A *kitchen scrub brush* for birdbaths and flowerpots will come in handy, as will a *dustbrush* for stepping stones and steps.

❦ A large *trash bag* for non-recyclable litter. Hang it where it is within easy reach as you work.

Week One

Week Two

Week Three

Week Four

year one MARCH

Week One

Week Two

Week Three

_____

_____

_____

_____

_____

_____

_____

_____

_____

_____

_____

Growing Plants from Seed

Few things say spring as clearly as seeds sprouting on the windowsill. If you have always wanted to try growing your own plants from seed indoors, here is how to get going. Don't forget to keep track of your seed-planting in your garden journal.

- Choose seeds from a catalog or a nursery; it is best to start with seeds marked "easy to grow." Although everything looks tempting, try to limit yourself to one or two packs at first.
- Gather your supplies: new small peat or plastic pots; a waterproof tray; soilless growing mix; and clear plastic wrap. You can also buy very inexpensive plastic greenhouse trays. To avoid plant diseases, it is most important to use new supplies.
- Arrange the pots in rows in the tray, and fill them almost to the top with the growing mix. Moisten slowly with lukewarm water. Make sure the mix is fully moistened and then drain off excess water.

Week Four

_____

_____

_____

_____

_____

_____

_____

_____

_____

_____

_____

_____

_____

🦋 Pour the seeds into a saucer. Use a paring knife to press two seeds into each pot. Cover with soil, if directed, and enclose the tray with the plastic wrap; hold the plastic above the soil with popsicle sticks or pencils. Place the tray in the light and temperature conditions noted on the seed package.

🦋 Remove the plastic after most seeds have germinated, and check the soil's moisture at least once a day. When the seedlings have two sets of leaves, use a small scissors to cut off the weaker seedling in each pot.

🦋 When weather permits, harden off the plants by moving them to a protected place outdoors for a few days before planting.

ANNUALS.

Morning Glory
Ipomoea Tricolor

Week One

MAY

year
one

Week Two

year one MAY

Week Three

Week Four

year one MAY

Week One

Week Two

year one JUNE

Week Three

Week Four

_____
_____
_____
_____
_____
_____
_____
_____
_____
_____
_____
_____
_____
_____
_____
_____
_____

year one JULY

A Color Theme Garden for the Shade

A shady garden offers an exciting challenge to your creativity. While it cannot be denied that many of our showiest perennials, such as peonies and bearded irises, are uncompromising sun lovers, a wealth of marvelous, colorful plants awaits the gardener in shade.

For maximum impact, consider the possibility of making a shade garden with a monochromatic color scheme. This can be done most effectively if you choose white, yellow, or blue as your theme color. A white garden sparkles even in shade, and lights up the darkest corner. Yellow is, of course, the color of sunshine, and your yellow shade garden will feel sunny,

Week Two

although it is not. Blue is cool and mysterious; it beckons and soothes. You cannot go wrong with any of these choices.

Make hostas the backbone of this garden. Dozens of enticing hostas feature foliage of green and white, green and yellow, or blue-green. Such hostas come in many sizes and leaf forms, and seeking out new specimens in your color scheme is a pleasurable pursuit.

As you plan your color theme garden, thumb through gardening magazines and reference books, and visit local gardens to discover shade plants in your color range. To maximize interest, make sure to choose plants with a variety of texture and form, as well as those that bloom in several different shades of the same color.

Week Three

Week Four

Week One

Week Two

year
one AUGUST

Week Three

Week Four

Week One

Week Two

Week Three

Week Four

Week One

Autumn Bounty for Indoor Decoration

Bringing your garden's beauty indoors is one of the special pleasures of gardening. There is no season of the year in which this is truer than autumn. From summer's end through the brisk days of November, it is not difficult to make your home reflect the glowing colors of nature's last hurrah.

What sort of materials can you use? You may want to begin with late-blooming perennials such as asters, chrysanthemums, and goldenrods. Many gardeners also like to go into their gardens the day before frost is predicted to gather one last glorious bouquet of annuals. But flowers are only the beginning. Consider the beauty of seedheads and pods. Coneflowers and baptisia are just two examples of perennials with such attractive assets. Take a look along the roadside. Many common wildflowers, including Queen Anne's lace and milkweed, have dispersed their seed,

Week Two

leaving seedheads and open pods that will enhance indoor wreaths and arrangements.

Autumn leaves evoke the season perhaps more than any of its other features. In some areas, the parade of changing leaves goes on for two months or more. Bring in branches of leaves as they turn, replacing them as they drop and others reach their peak. In addition to trees and shrubs, remember that many perennials, such as amsonia, have spectacular autumn coloring.

No autumn arrangement is complete without berries, which symbolize the bounty of the season. Garden shrubs, such as viburnums, and numerous wild plants offer many possibilities. If you have small children or pets, however, do not bring berries indoors unless you know they are safe.

What can you do with the riches of autumn? Fill vases large and small, decorate wreaths and swags, make napkin rings, scatter them on the table, and enjoy the largesse of another season in your garden.

Week Three

Week Four

Week One

Week Two

Week Three

Week Four

Week One

Week Two

year one DECEMBER

Week Three

Week Four

Year

_____

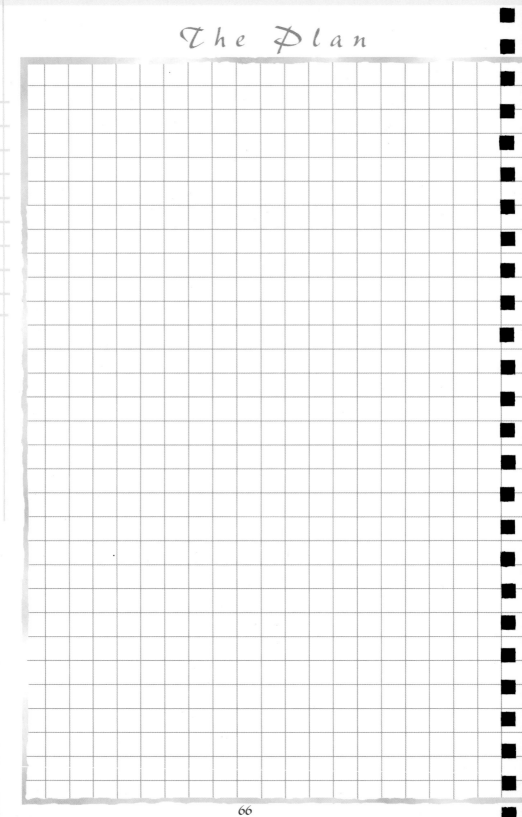

Week One

Week Two

Week Three

_____

_____

_____

_____

_____

_____

_____

_____

_____

_____

Plants for Winter Interest

Winter can be a season of serene and restful beauty in your garden, no matter how frigid the weather. In much of North America, it is in this time of spare simplicity that the bones of our gardens are most evident. The framework of the garden— its hedges and trees, pathways and ornaments— reveals itself in a special way. In this quiet season, you can use your garden journal to plan changes as you contemplate your winter garden.

Well-chosen plants will enhance the winter garden. The front of your house, significant views from indoors, and frequently used areas such as the back door should include plants with winter interest. Consider the following factors as you plan your garden.

Week Four

❧ *Evergreens,* the stalwarts of the winter garden, are usually categorized as needled or broadleaved. To find out what grows well in your area, talk to other gardeners in your community, visit public gardens with labeled plants, and read books and magazines.

❧ *Bark,* often forgotten by gardeners, is one of the most outstanding features of the winter landscape. Shrubs and trees that offer colored or exfoliating bark add a unique dimension to the garden.

❧ *Berries* and *seedheads* are ornamental, and are wonderful for holiday decorating. In addition, they attract birds to the garden, giving it life and zest in the depth of winter.

❧ *Branch structure* can make a tree or shrub an outstanding feature of your garden. A few plants possess good branch structure naturally; most have to be helped along by pruning. Study your shrubs and trees as if each were a piece of sculpture, as indeed it is. From such contemplation, the true art of the garden emerges.

Week One

year two

Week Two

FEBRUARY

year two

Week Three

Week Four

Week One

Week Two

Week Three

_____

_____

_____

_____

_____

_____

_____

_____

_____

_____

_____

_____

_____

Transplanting and Dividing

Spring is the ideal time for transplanting and dividing plants, although gardeners in hot climates may prefer to take care of this task in autumn. Note during the growing season plants that should be moved or divided. Then you can attend to the task in the cool weather of early spring, as soon as new growth appears.

A wise old New England gardener, Katherine Taylor, once commented, "You can do what you want in your own garden." This tart remark certainly applies to transplanting. It is gentler on the plant to move it in early spring but, if you are careful about after-care, feel free to move most plants whenever it is convenient for you.

Week Four

Dig the new hole first, a little deeper and wider than the root ball. Have a supply of compost and fresh soil nearby. Shovel a mixture of the two into the hole. Slice through the soil in a circle around the plant. Lift the plant out of the ground and move it to its new position. Fill around the root ball with the soil and compost mix. Press your foot firmly around the plant to settle air pockets. Water attentively for the rest of the growing season, and provide shade if the plant is in full leaf when moved.

Dividing plants is similar. When the plant is out of the ground, slice it into sections with a spade. Discard old woody growth that may be present in plants such as chrysanthemums. Replant vigorously growing sections and provide the same aftercare described for transplants.

Week One

Week Two

Week Three

Week Four

Week One

Week Two

Week Three

Week Four

Week One

_____
_____
_____
_____
_____
_____
_____
_____
_____
_____
_____

Creative Container Gardening

One of the pleasures of spring is planning your containers. Whether you
have many acres in a rural area or the tiniest city balcony, containers offer a
place to try new plants and new combinations every year. You can even
change your plantings as the seasons progress. And, of course, the containers themselves offer endless possibilities.

Begin by deciding where you would like to feature container plantings.
The best rule is to put them where you will see them frequently, and
where you can easily care for them. Entrances, decks, and terraces are perfect choices. Window boxes and garden focal points are also appropriate.
You may prefer, however, to surprise people. A container on a pedestal
in a perennial border is an eye-catching feature that lends height to
the composition.

What should you use for a container? The classics include terra-cotta
pots, wood structures ranging from high-style Versailles boxes to rain bar-

Week Two

rels, and interpretations in concrete of antique stone. Lead and cast-iron are also traditional. But do not be afraid to be unconventional. Make your garden exciting and expressive of your personality.

Fill containers with fresh soil every year. Plants in such small spaces quickly use up soil nutrients. Old soil can be added to your compost pile.

The list of plants for containers is almost endless, from annuals, perennials, herbs, and vegetables to shrubs, vines, and even trees. Dare to experiment. Compose a picture of many plants of one color, for instance, or an interesting interplay of textures. Include different forms, vertical, mounding, trailing.

After planting, mulch containers to keep the soil's moisture and temperature even. Fertilize frequently with a liquid fertilizer, especially for annuals. At the end of the growing season, plant in your garden anything that will not winter over in the container. And begin to think about the exciting possibilities for next year!

Week Three

Week Four

Week One

"Roses climb everywhere"

Week Two

Week Three

year
two

Week Four

Week One

Week Two

Week Three

Week Four

Week One

Week Two

SEPTEMBER

year two

Week Three

Week Four

year two SEPTEMBER

Week One

Week Two

Week Three

Week Four

Week One

_____
_____
_____
_____
_____
_____
_____
_____
_____
_____
_____
_____
_____

Bulbs

Autumn reinvigorates the gardener, and one of the season's pleasures is planting bulbs. Each bulb, settled in rich, brown earth, is a promise that spring will come again. The quality of the bulbs you plant now, however, is the key to the beauty of your spring garden—be sure to buy from a reputable nursery or catalog.

With a few exceptions, most bulbs want soil of average fertility and moisture. They do not like wet soil, and must have full sun to ripen their foliage. Shade will diminish or eliminate the next year's flowers. Bulb foliage must be left to ripen naturally before it is removed. The foliage cannot be cut off, braided, or twisted to hide this ripening process, so plant your

Week Two

bulbs where the ripening foliage will not detract from the beauty of your garden as the pageant of later bloom unfolds. Best flowering will occur with a light application of ordinary 5-10-5 fertilizer at the time of planting, when the bulbs first appear in spring, and after the flowers have gone by.

While planting your bulbs this autumn, take care to note their location in your garden journal. Next spring, it will be helpful to add a few comments on their performance. Do not hesitate to remove those you did not care for and to increase the number of types you liked. It is just this refining process that will help your garden to become more beautiful each year. And don't forget to try something new each autumn. If you have always grown the glorious Darwin tulips, for instance, why not try a few of the very early species tulips this year?

List in your garden journal what you have planted this autumn, as well as bulbs you might like to try in the future.

NOVEMBER

year two

Week Three

Week Four

Week One

Week Two

Week Three

Week Four

The Garden's Design

An organized garden design process will make all the difference in the beauty of your garden and the satisfaction it can offer you. Your garden journal is the place to plan that process in simple steps. First, you will look at your garden space, large or small, and its unique characteristics. Then, you will look at yourself and what you want your garden to do. Finally, you will play freely with ideas until you decide which design works best for you and your garden. This process holds true for the tiniest flower garden as well as for a country place of many acres.

YOUR GARDEN SPACE

Let's begin with your land. Landscape designers call this part of the process the "site analysis." Included here are some important points to note in your garden journal, but feel free to choose those that are most relevant to your own garden.

Use the graph pages at the start of each year to sketch your garden with the significant features described here. You can do this freehand by approximating distances, or you may prefer to take measurements outside and use a ruler to create an exact scale drawing. If you like, you can also note this information in written form on the blank pages provided. Choose the method that is most comfortable for you. As you make your sketches and notes, make sure to observe the following:

- What is the size of the garden? Measure your space.
- Where are north, south, east, and west?
- What areas are sunny or shady? Are there places that are too sunny or too shady and need modifying?
- Are there places that get a lot of wind or have poor air circulation?
- Are there noise or odor problems to solve?
- What are the soil's characteristics, its texture and organic content? Is it acid or alkaline, sandy or heavy with clay? If you are uncertain, ask a neighbor who is an experienced gardener or contact your county extension service.
- Is your garden space hilly or flat? Is erosion a problem?
- Do you have a stream or a pond?
- Is water readily available for dry spells, or do you live where water is scarce?
- Is your soil particularly wet or dry in places?
- What and where are the plants that will remain, from the largest tree to the smallest wildflower? What plants are to be removed?
- What is the "feel" of the surrounding landscape: country, suburban, city? Do you wish to harmonize with the landscape or create a counterpoint with a style quite different?
- What is the architectural style of your house? Do you want your garden to blend harmoniously with this style or to make a bold statement of contrast?
- Are there outdoor structures such as a terrace or swimming pool?
- Do you have children who need play areas?
- Do you have pets that will run free in the garden? Are there wild animals to be considered, such as deer or woodchucks?
- Do you have views you would like to emphasize, such as natural scenery, a neighbor's specimen birch, or a soaring white church steeple? Do you have views you wish to screen?
- What exists that cannot be changed, such as a driveway or town easement?

- What are the materials of your walks and driveway? Do you want to continue these in new construction?
- Is there something of historic or cultural significance about your property that should be taken into consideration?
- Where are your underground utilities? Examples include septic systems, water lines, wells, cable TV, gas, phone, and electricity.

Once you have recorded the details of what your garden is like now, you can move on to the next step, assessing your wishes and needs.

Your Garden Dreams

Your garden journal can help you record all the roles you would like your garden to play in your life. Some of these will be obvious to you without any further thought; others may surprise you as you read through the following list. Your garden journal is the place to record these individual goals. This part of the design process is called the "program."

- What is your favorite season of the year? Try to plan your garden to peak at that time. Even winter can be spectacular in a well-planned garden.
- Do you vacation at the same time each year? You will probably want to avoid plants that bloom unseen at that time.
- What kinds of plants do you want to grow? Examples include perennials, annuals, herbs, wildflowers, vegetables, shrubs with attractive flowers or foliage, dwarf evergreens, and specimen trees.
- Do you want a mixed garden of several categories of plants, such as perennials, annuals, and small flowering shrubs, or do you prefer a succession of special garden areas, each devoted to one theme, such as alpines?

- Are there qualities such as fragrance or shade that you want to bring into your garden?
- Do you dream of specialty gardens, such as a water garden or a glorious cutting garden for indoor flower arranging?
- How much time can you spend on gardening? How important is low maintenance?
- What is your garden budget?
- Do you prefer gardens with architectural form, such as squares, ovals, and axes, or a naturalistic style derived from meadows or woodlands, for example? Looking at photographs in garden magazines and books can help you decide what you like best.
- What kinds of garden ornaments do you like? Funky and "in your face"? Or classic and evocative of an ordered past?
- From what windows can you best see your garden? These views should receive your chief attention. Just looking at your garden is one of its most important uses.
- Do you plan to use your garden for entertaining?
- Is there a swimming pool or deck in your future, for which you need to leave room? What about a storage area for a boat or RV?
- Are you planning your garden to be a peaceful outdoor sanctuary, or do you expect it will be lively with sporting activities? Or both?
- Do you hope to attract birds and butterflies, and are you willing to live with the seedheads and other mild untidiness they require?
- What are your favorite colors? And those you may dislike? Color harmony is one of the secrets of any successful flower garden.
- What are your needs for wheelbarrow access, compost piles, and other garden maintenance requirements?
- Do you need to improve your circulation system, that is, how you, your family, and your friends move through the garden space?

These suggestions should give you a good idea of what is important to you about your garden, both as it exists now and as you hope it will become.

CREATING THE DESIGN: PUTTING IT ALL TOGETHER

Now that you have gathered and recorded information about your garden space as it is now and thought about the various roles you would like your garden to play in your life, it is time to create a plan to make those dreams come true.

Begin this part of the design process by brainstorming as many ideas as you can, from garden details to larger concepts, such as a new layout. Use a pad of paper either to sketch your ideas or to write them down, whichever is more comfortable for you. It is important to remain very loose and flexible at this point. Do not reject out of hand any idea that occurs to you. One of America's greatest garden writers, Mrs. Francis King, once said, "In gardening, always take a chance."

When you feel satisfied, concentrate on developing the most pleasing of your garden visions. Then record it on the graph pages that precede each year, working with the existing landscape you have already sketched. Again, you can do this freehand or to scale. If you prefer, you can write a description on the blank pages of your journal.

You will now have a plan that incorporates both existing conditions and dreams to be fulfilled. Enjoy the process!

Plant Record

Be sure to include your plants' botanical names, common names, and quantity purchased; you might also wish to note cost and place of purchase, when they flowered, colors of flowers or foliage, how they performed, and any special requirements.

Plant Name	#	Comments

Plant Name	#	Comments

Plant Name	#	Comments

Plant Name	#	Comments

Plant Name	#	Comments

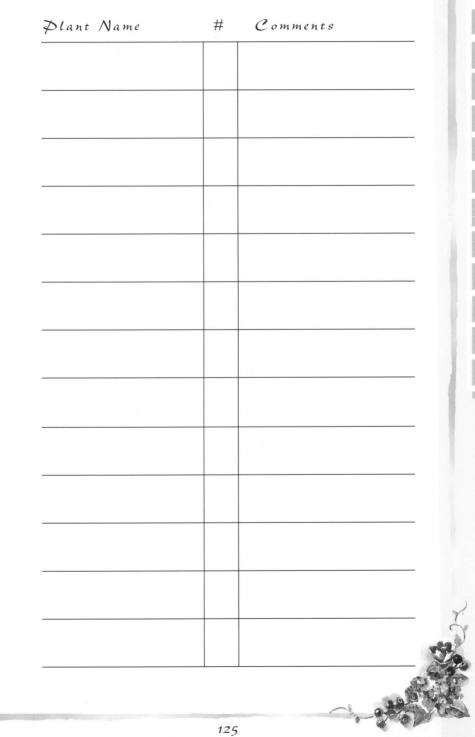

ADDRESSES

Note the addresses and phone numbers of your favorite garden suppliers
for easy reference.

PLANT HARDINESS ZONES

Range of Average
Annual Minimum
Temperatures for
Each Zone

	Fahrenheit (°F)	Celsius (°C)
ZONE 1	BELOW -50°	BELOW -45.6°
ZONE 2	-50° TO -40°	-45.6° TO -40°
ZONE 3	-40° TO -30°	-40° TO -34.4°
ZONE 4	-30° TO -20°	-34.4° TO -28.9°
ZONE 5	-20° TO -10°	-28.9° TO -23.3°
ZONE 6	-10° TO 0°	-23.3° TO -17.8°
ZONE 7	0° TO 10°	-17.8° TO -12.2°
ZONE 8	10° TO 20°	-12.2° TO -6.7°
ZONE 9	20° TO 30°	-6.7° TO -1.1°
ZONE 10	30° TO 40°	-1.1° TO 4.4°
ZONE 11	ABOVE 40°	ABOVE 4.4°

If you are living outside
North America, use the chart
to determine your Plant Hardiness Zone.